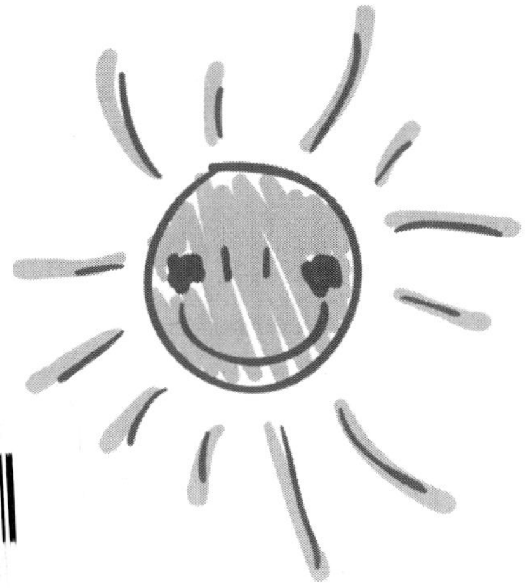

This journal belongs to

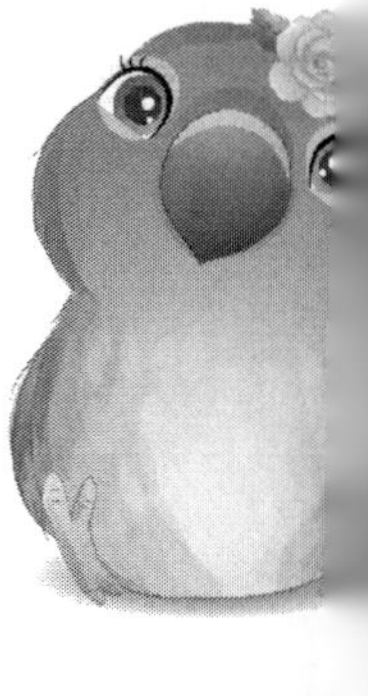

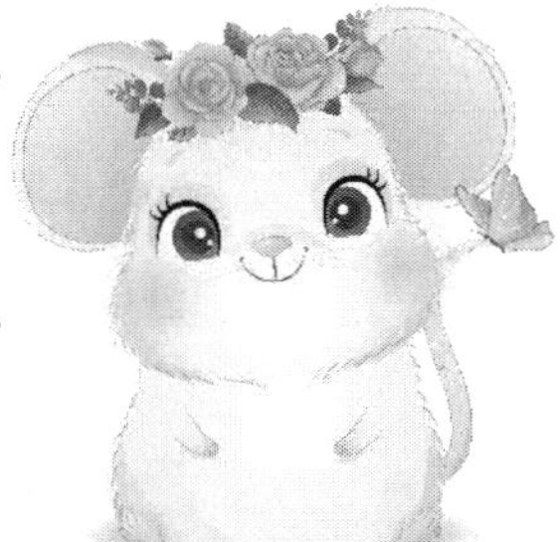

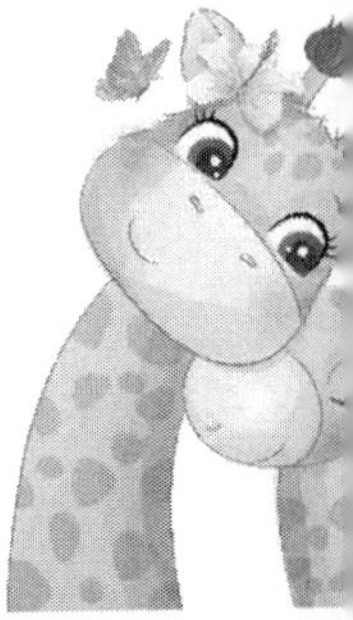

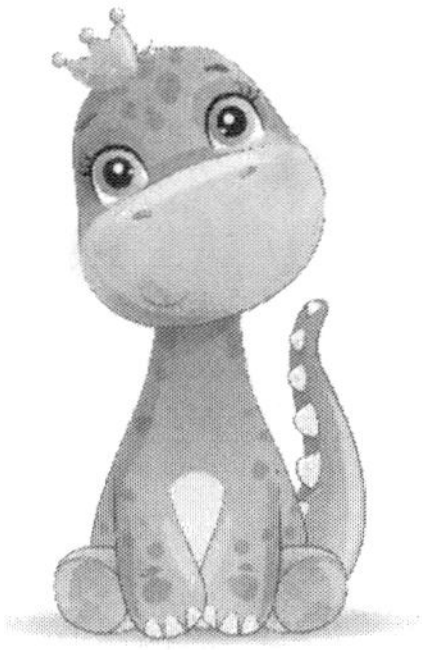

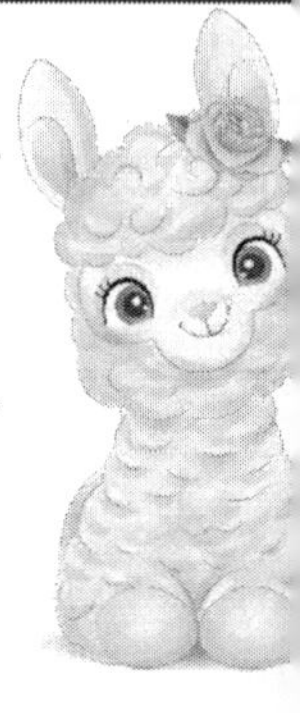

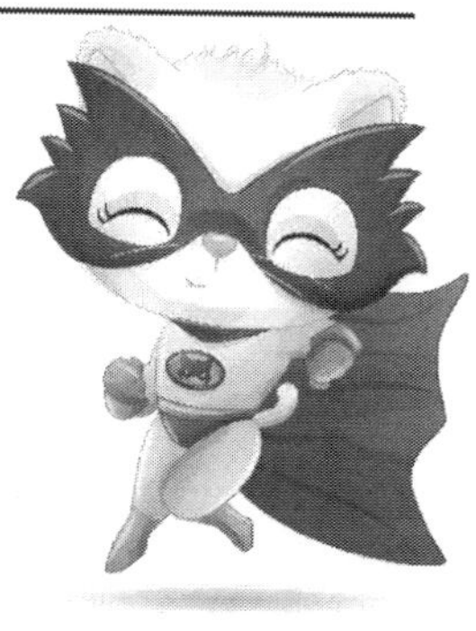

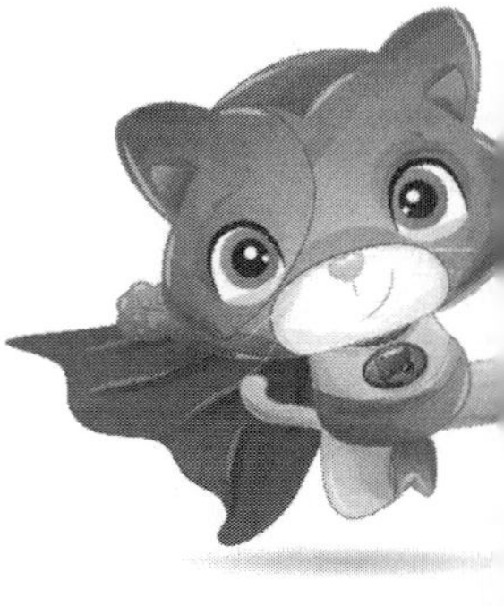

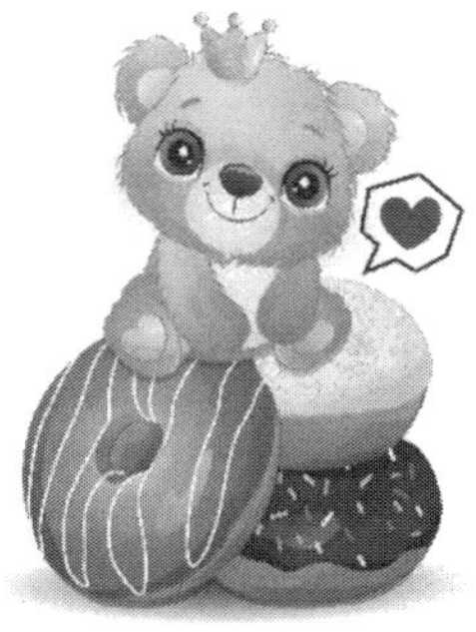

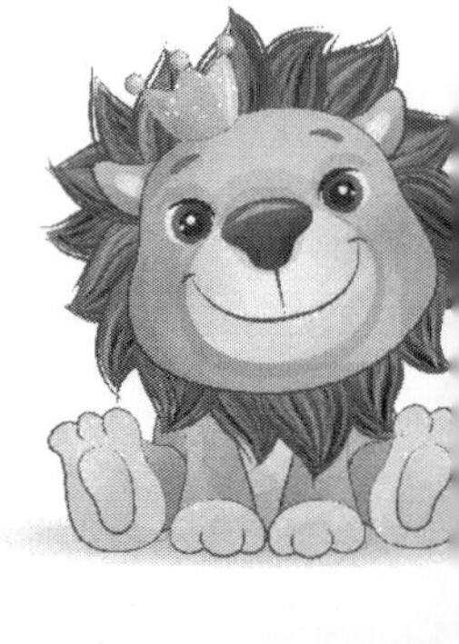

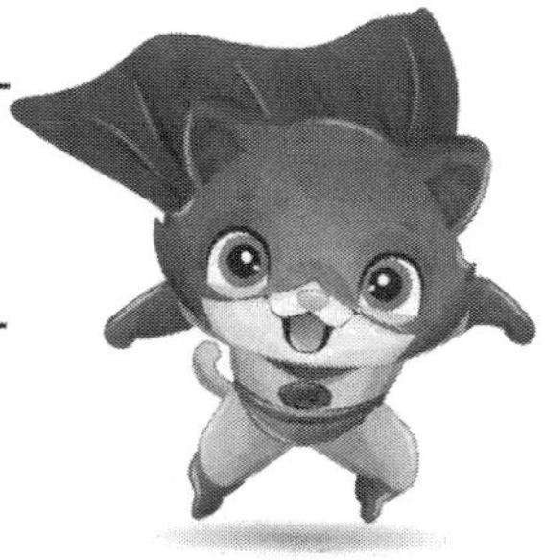

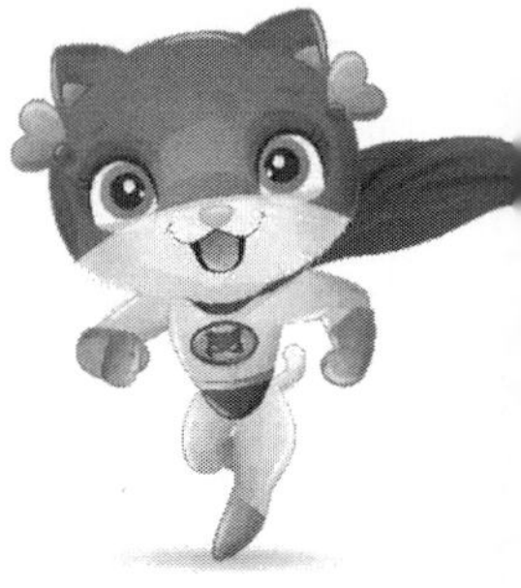

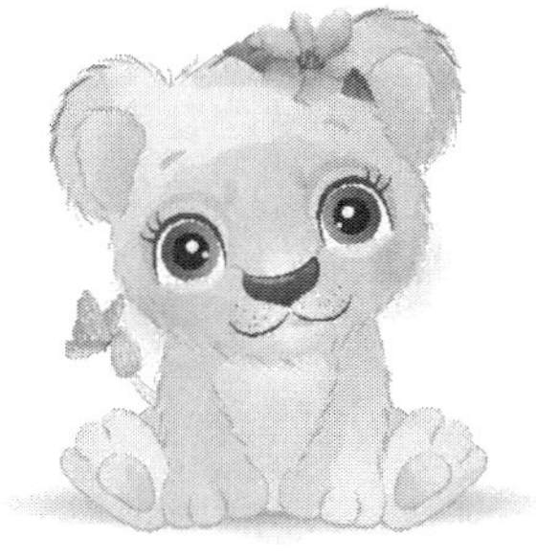

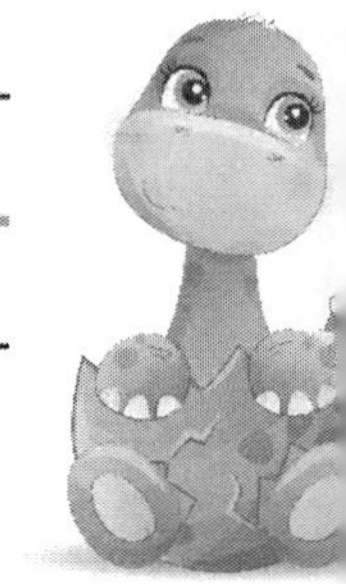

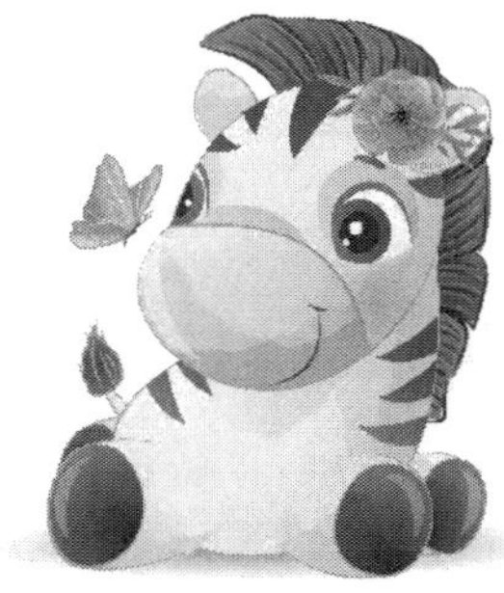

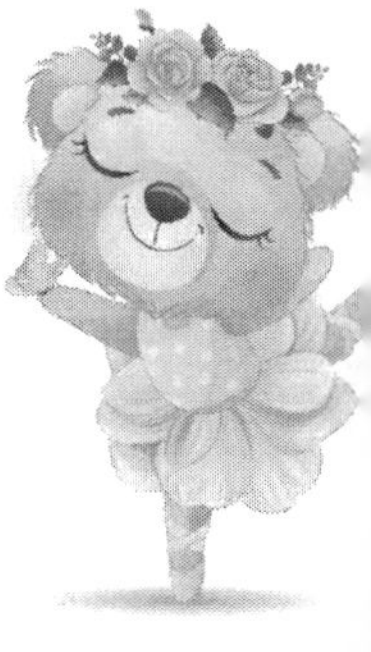

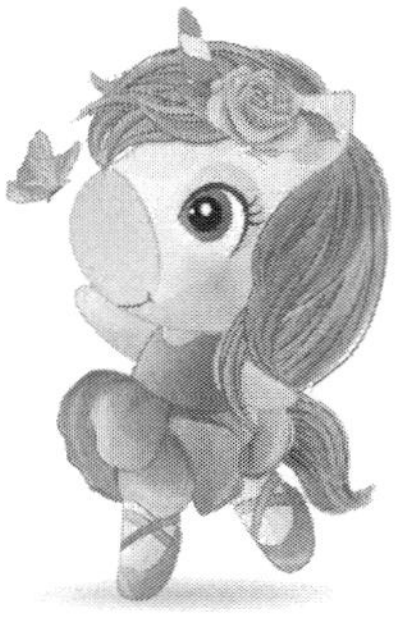

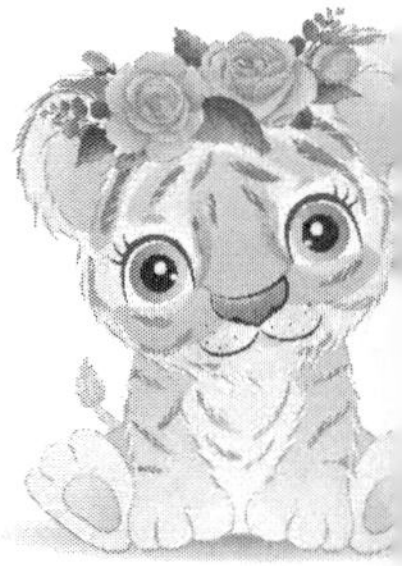

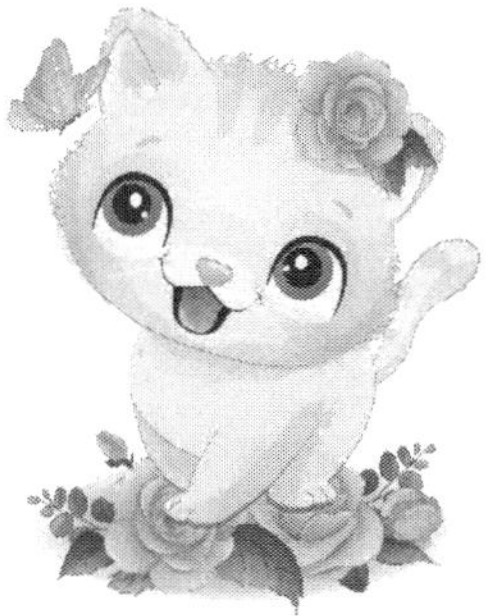

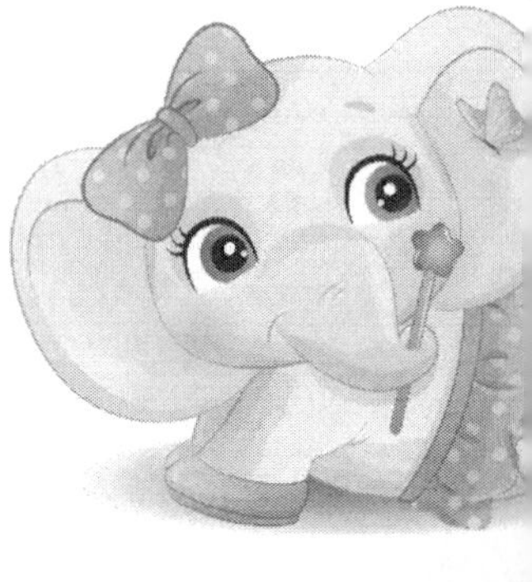

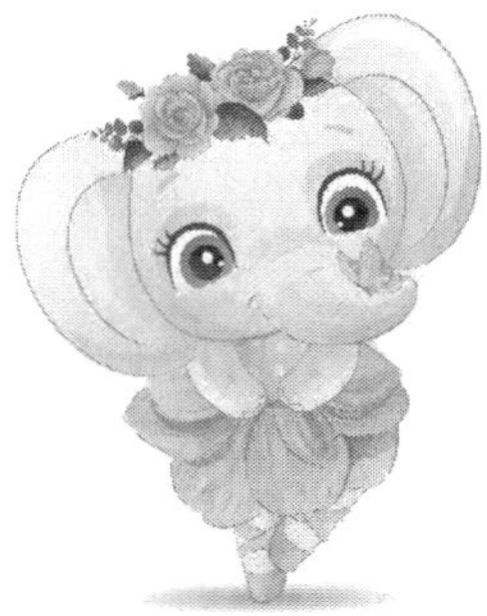

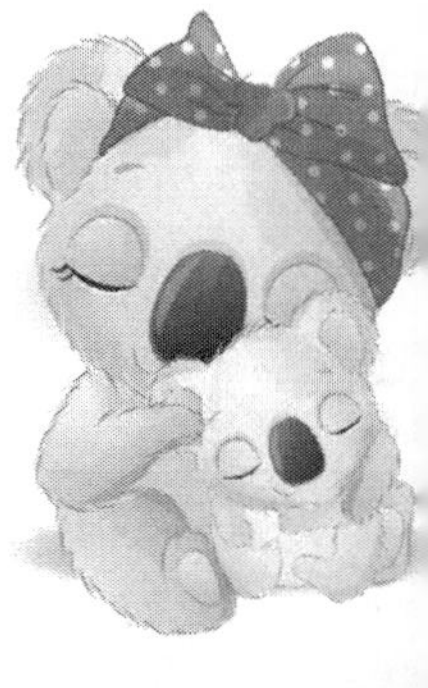

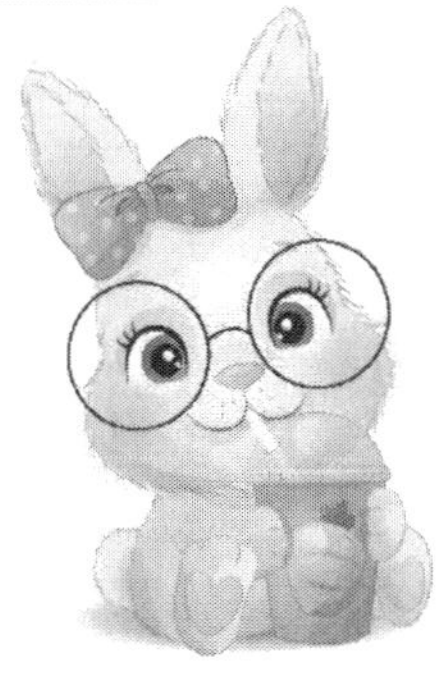

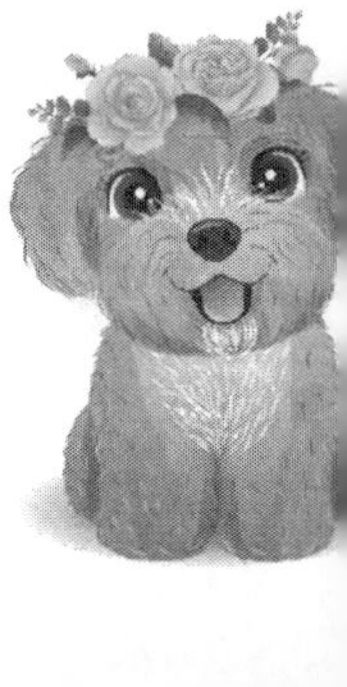

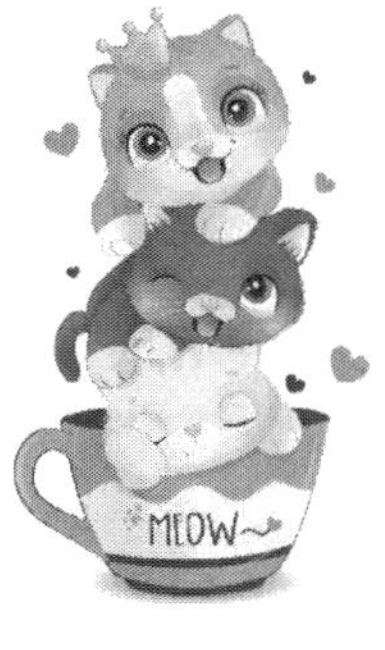
MEOW~

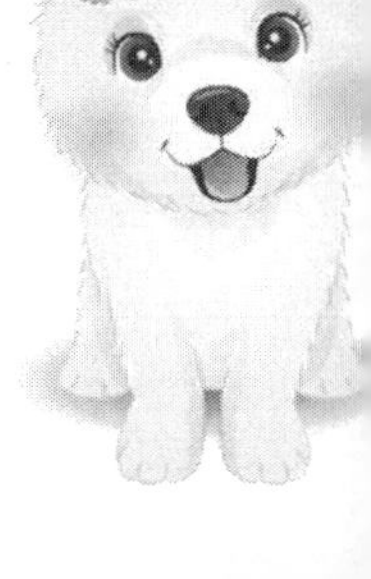

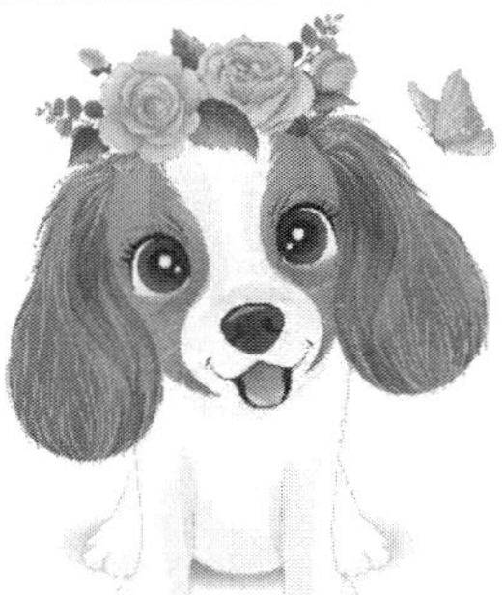

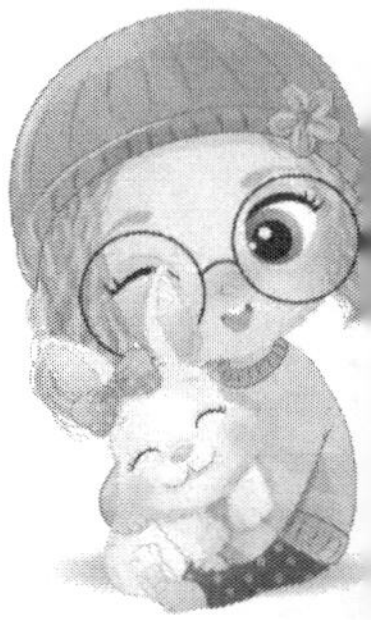

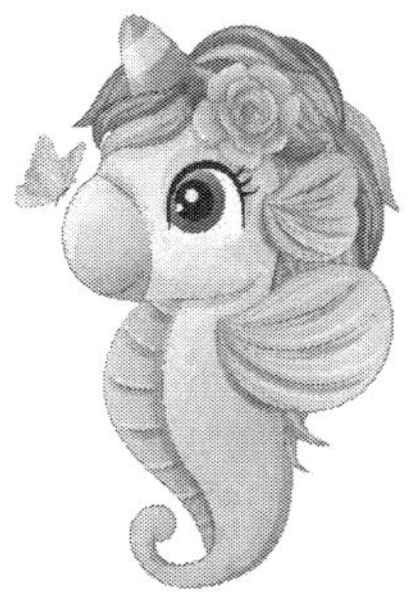

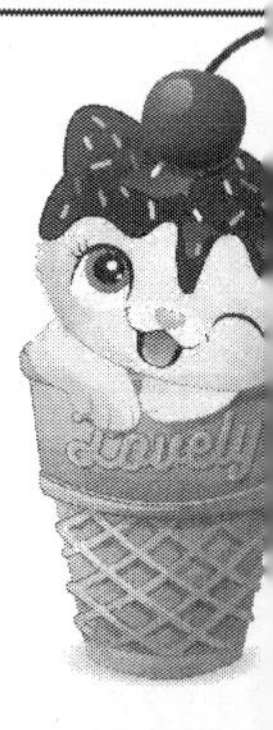

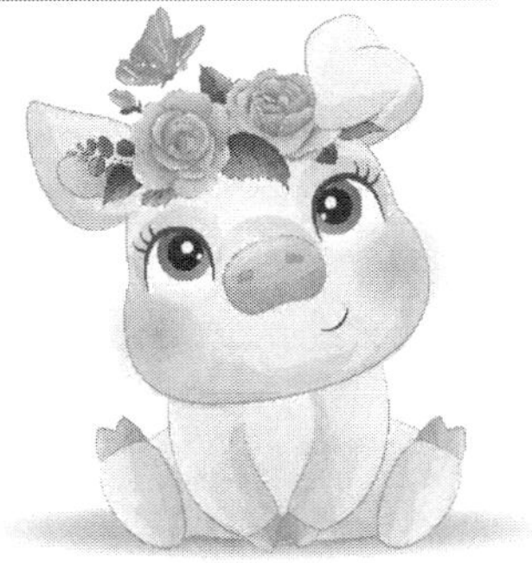

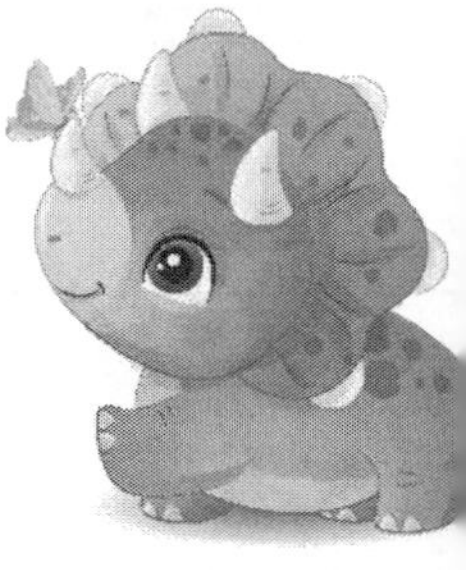

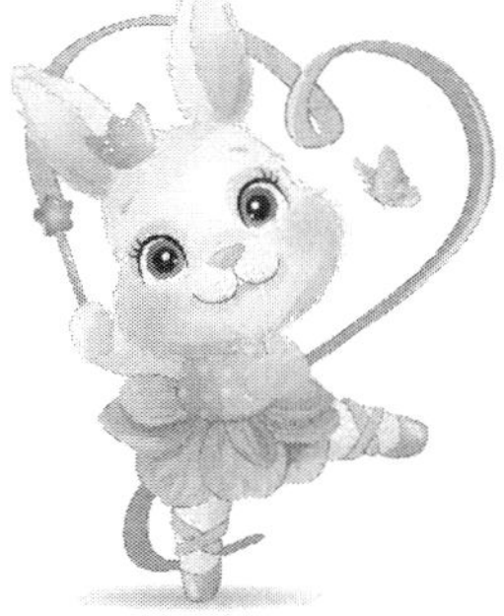

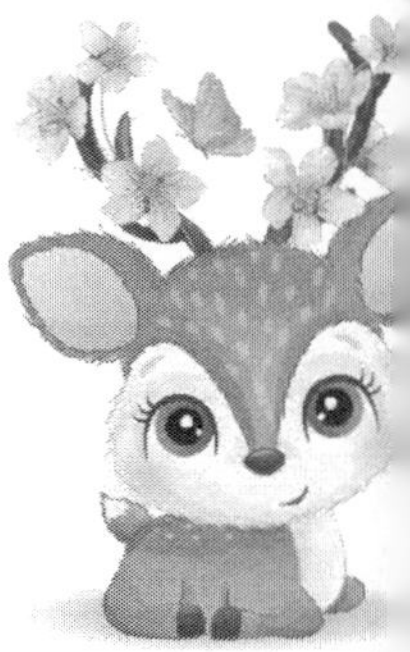

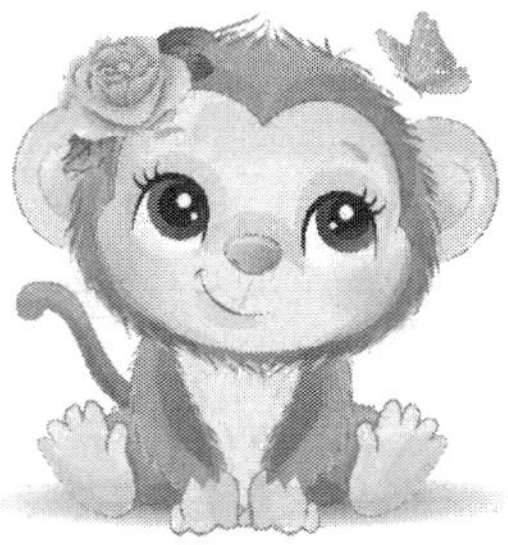

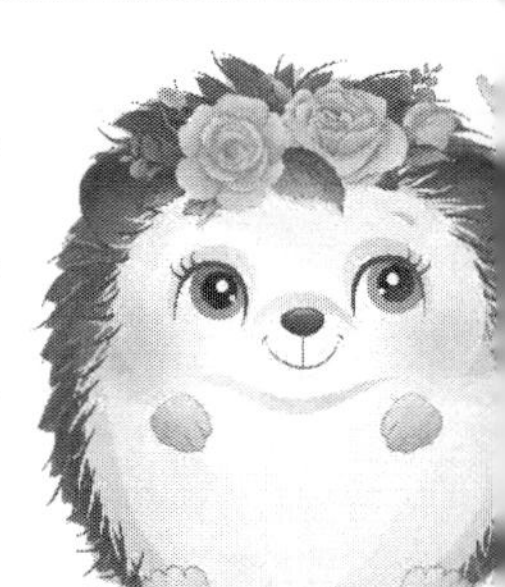

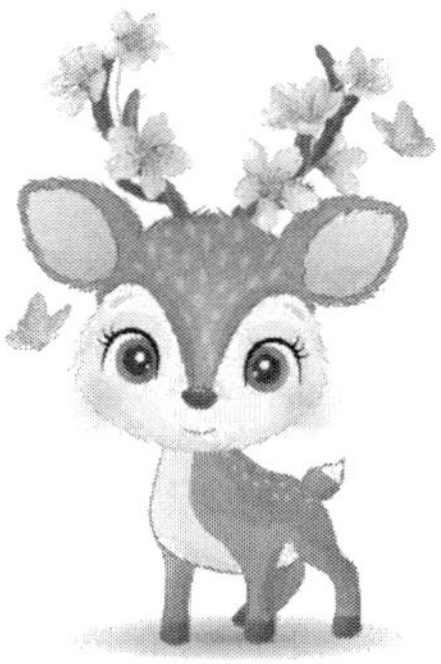

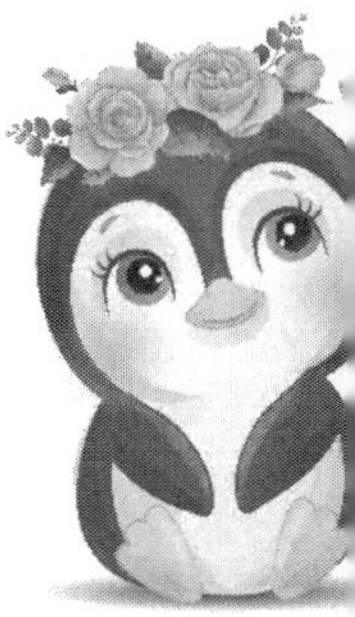

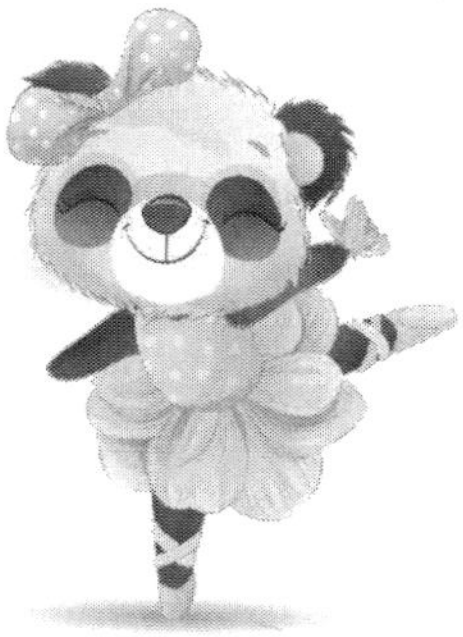

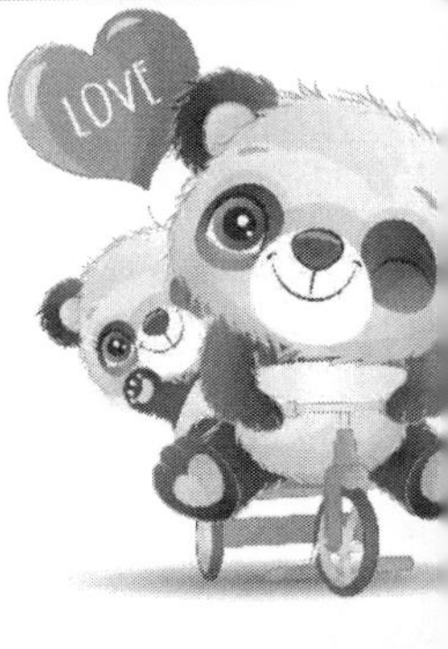
LOVE

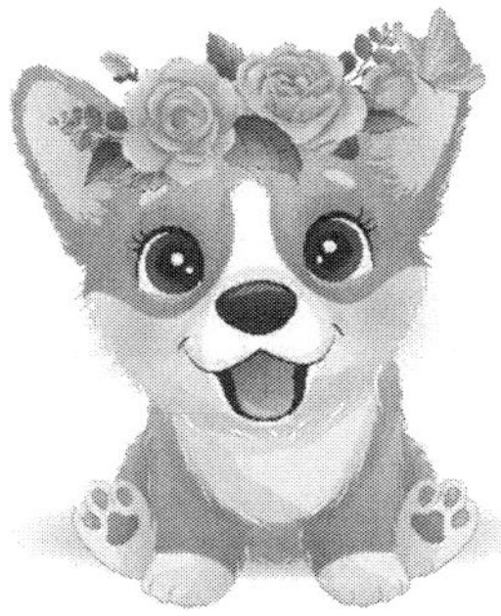

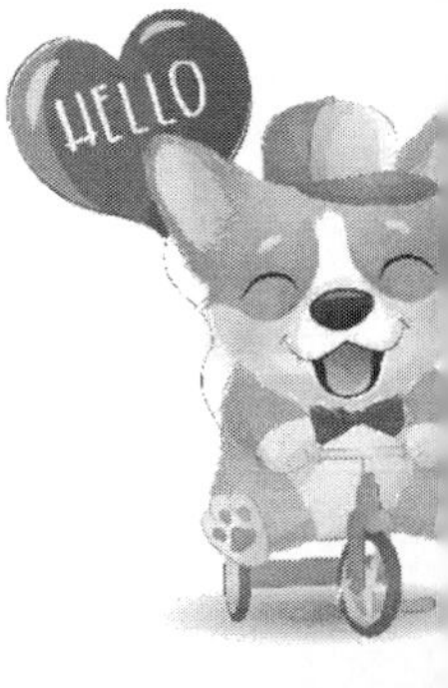
HELLO

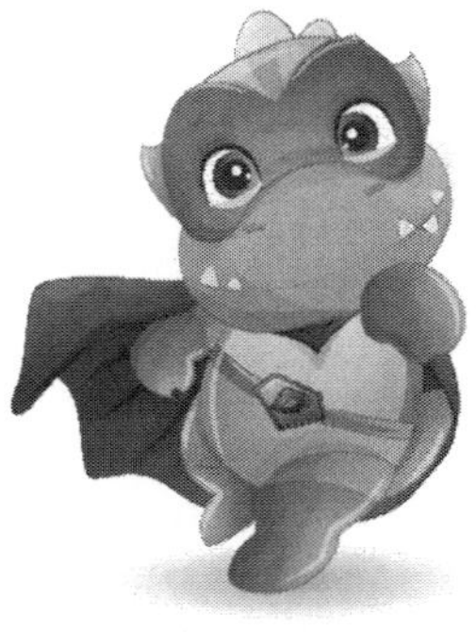

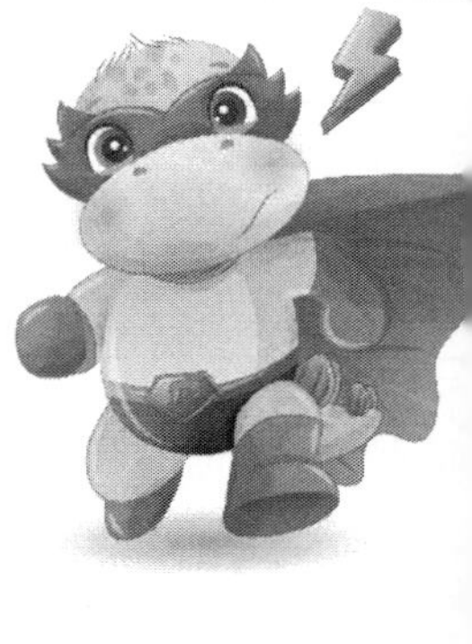

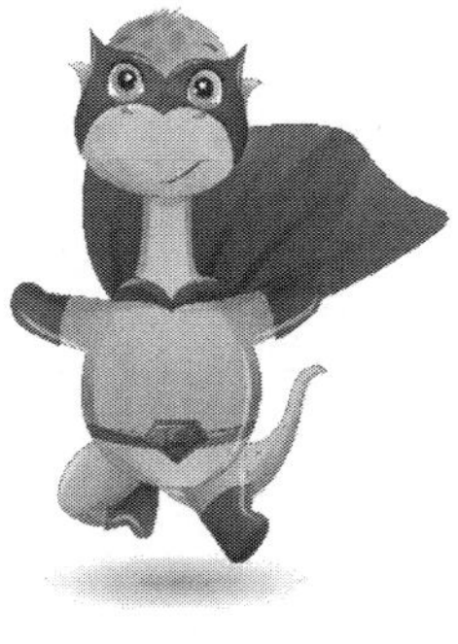

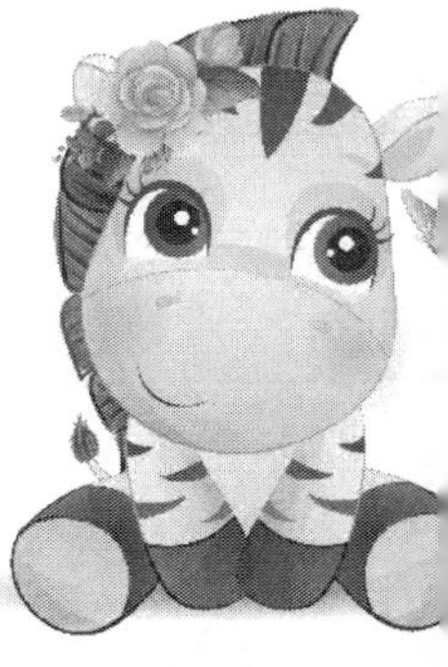

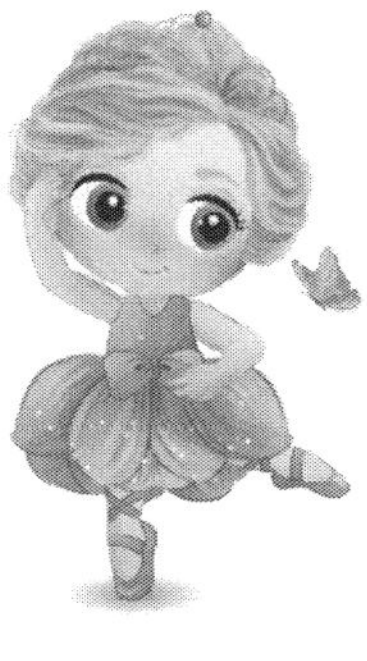

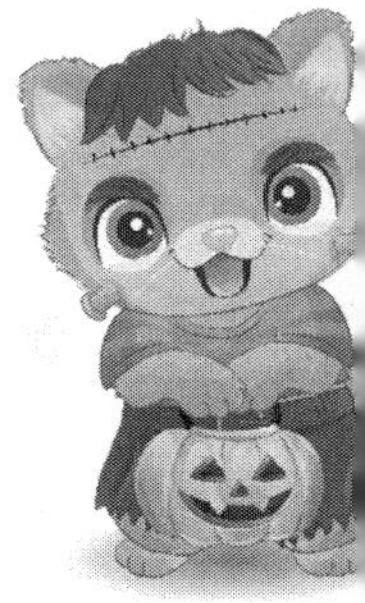

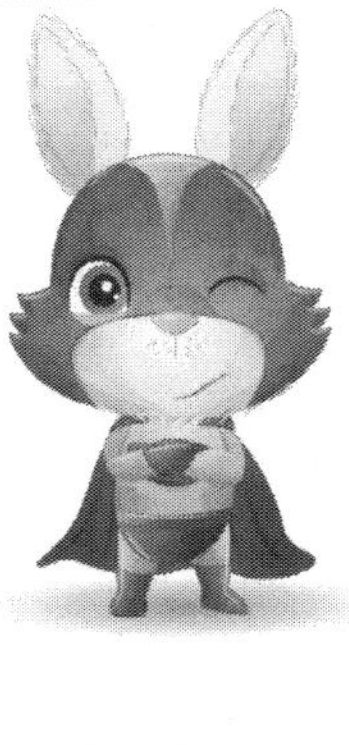

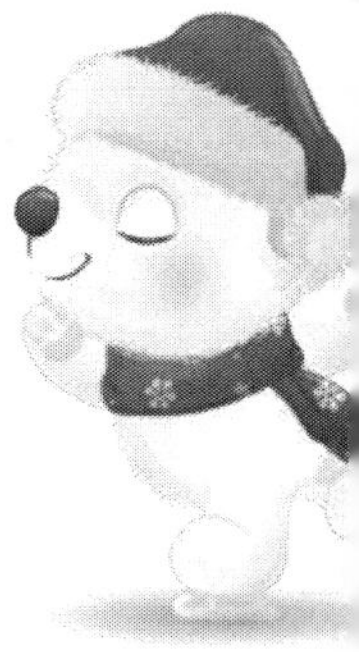

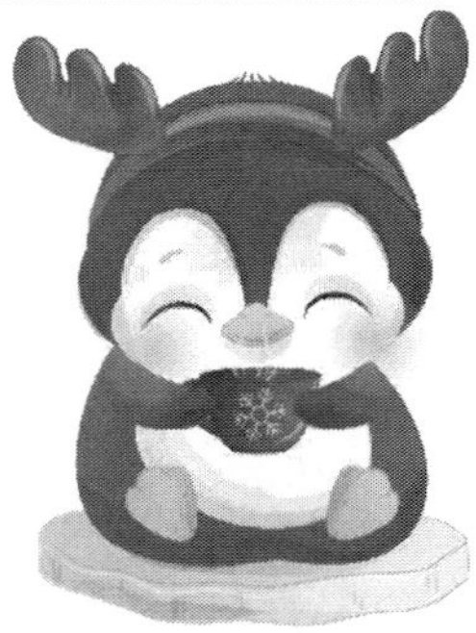

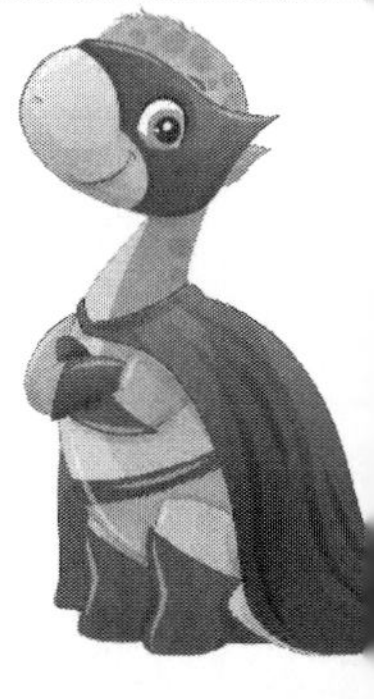

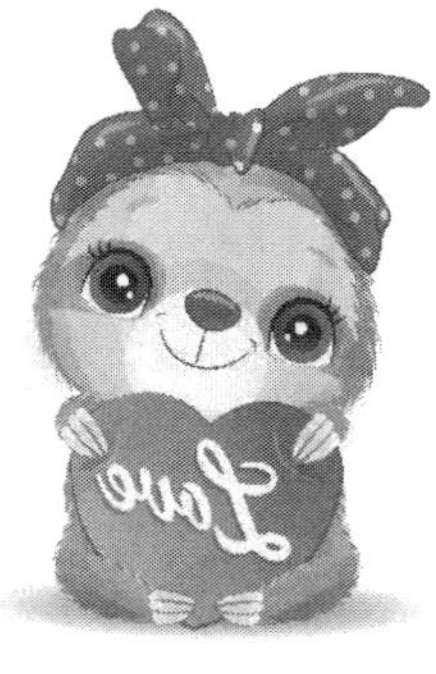
Love

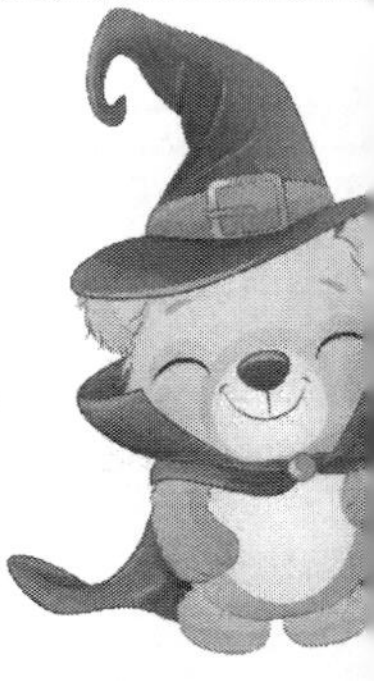

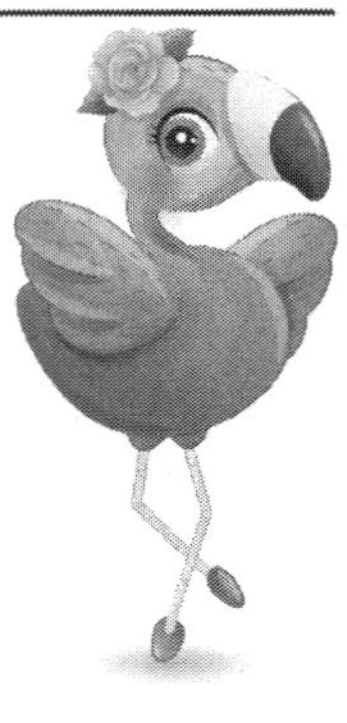

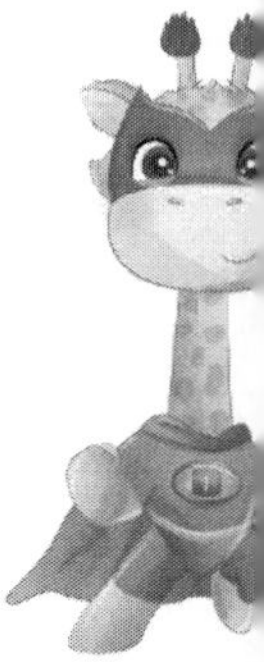

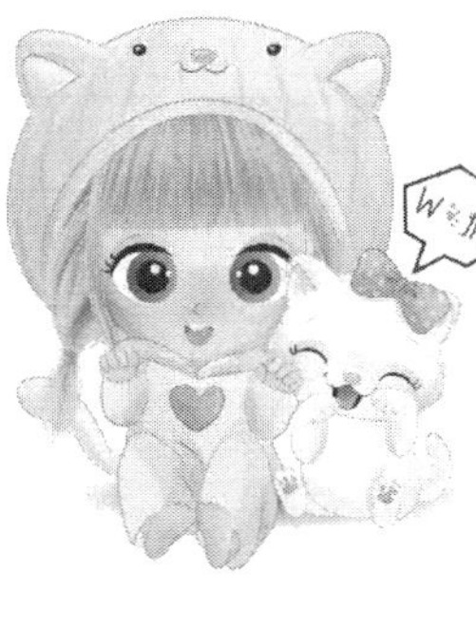

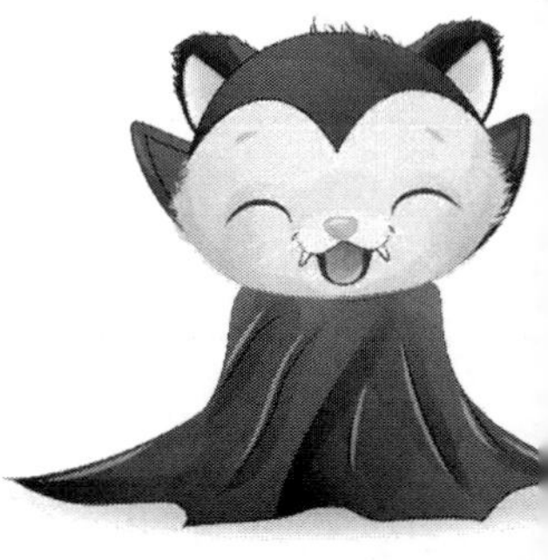

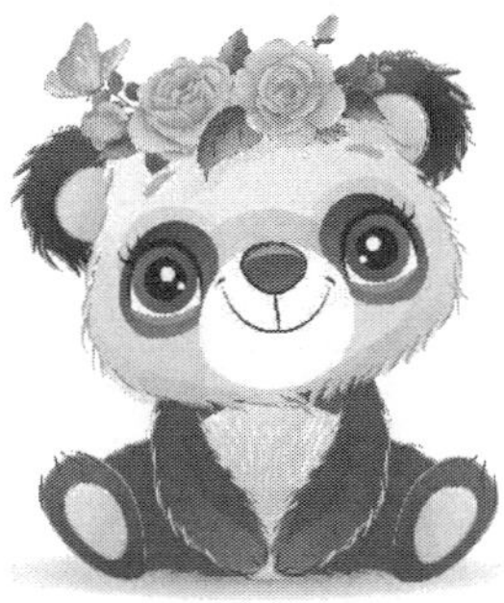

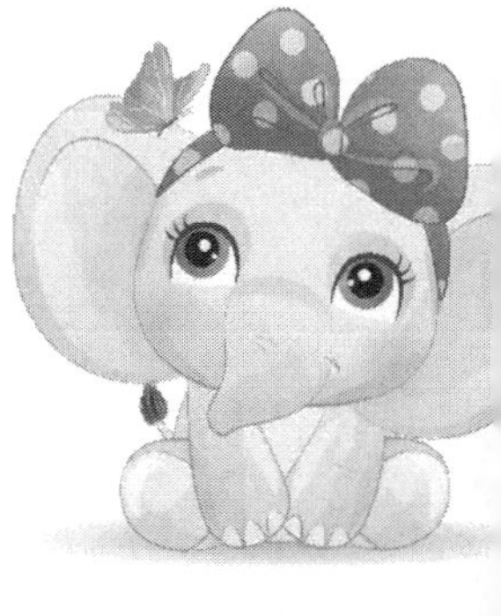

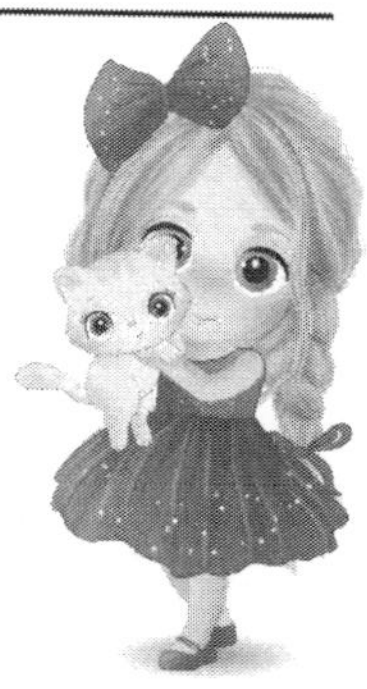

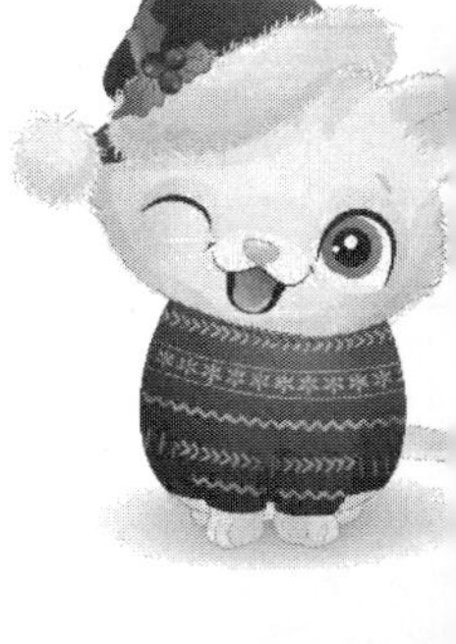

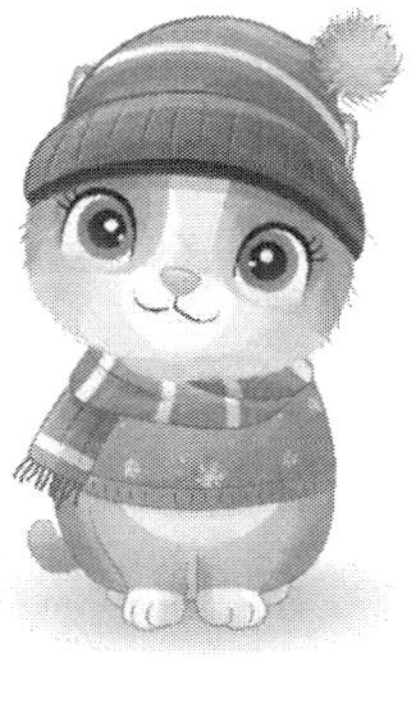

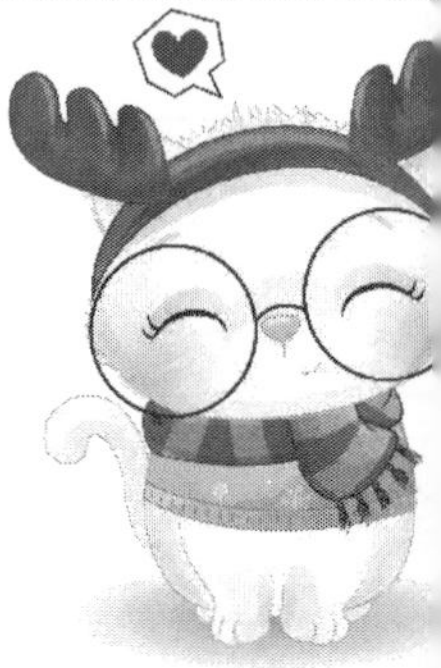

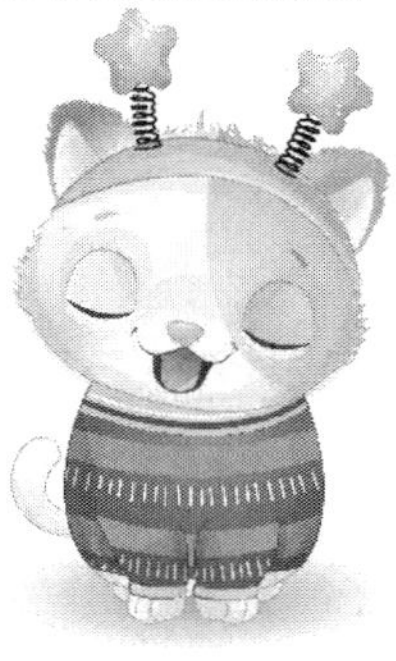

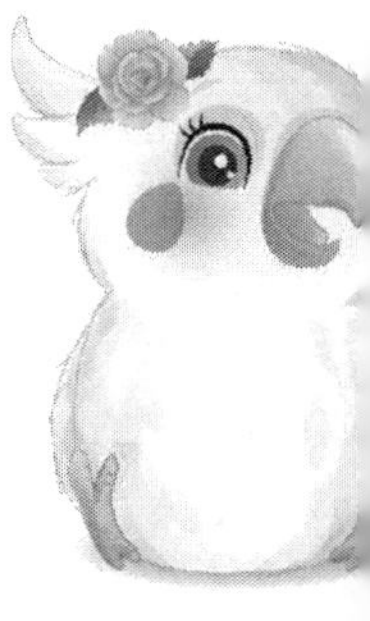

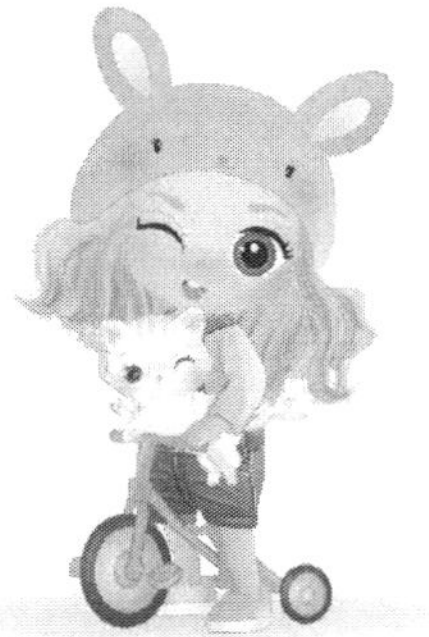

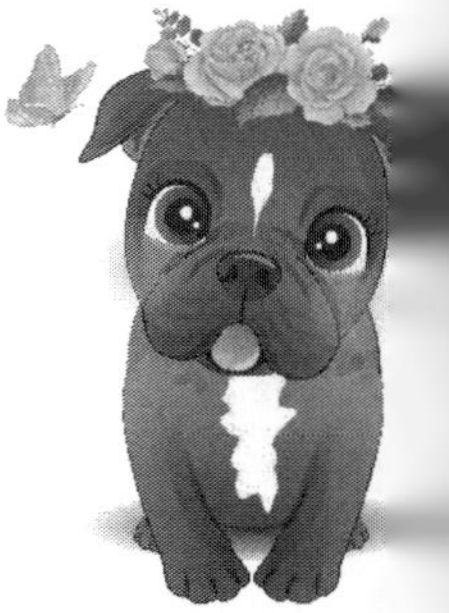

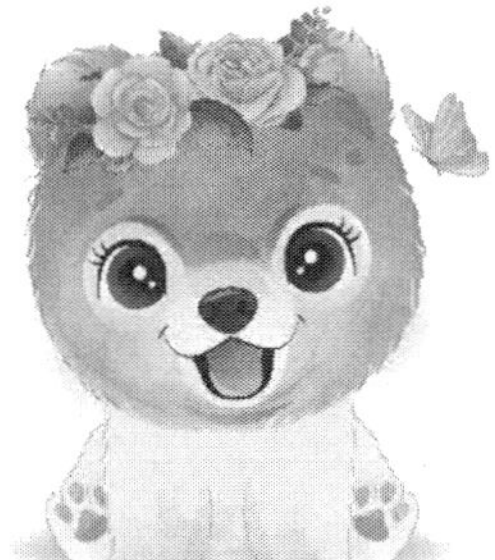

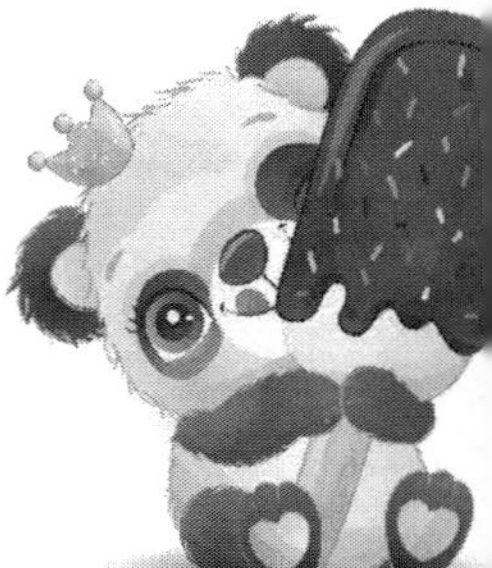

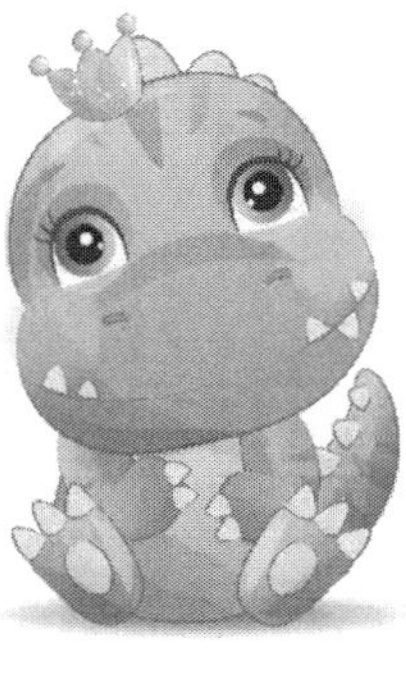

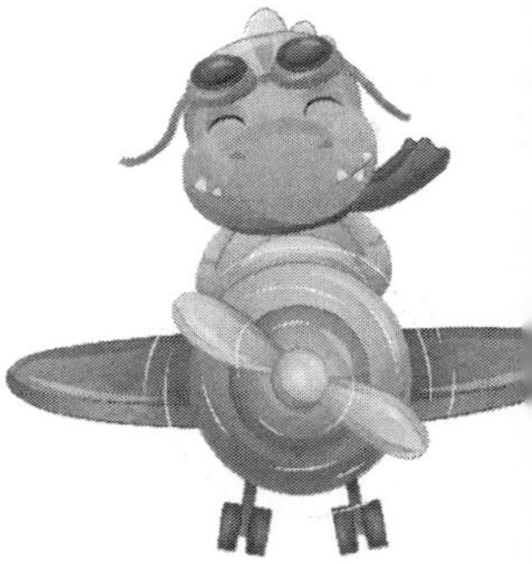

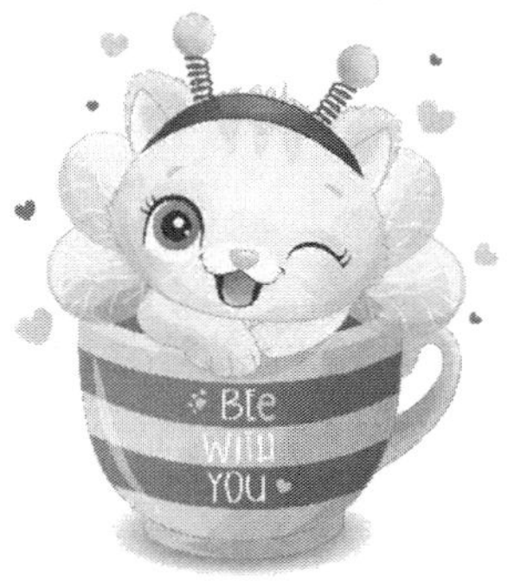
Bee
With
You

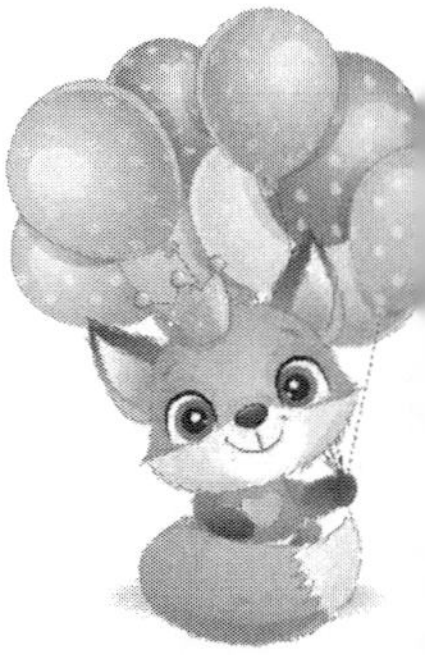

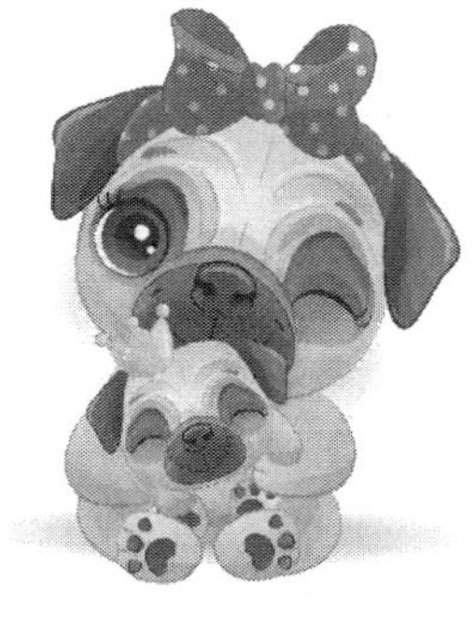

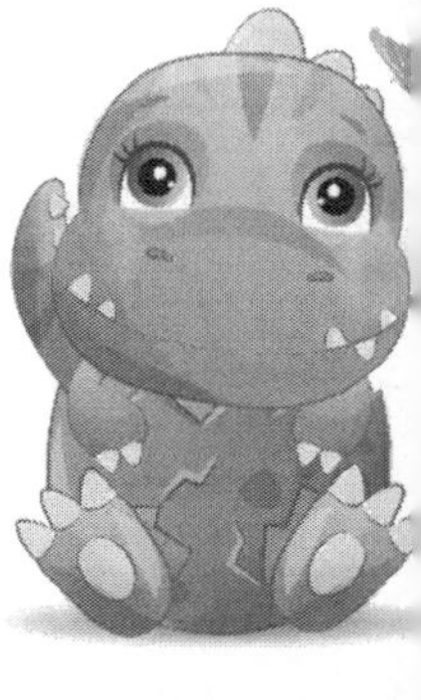

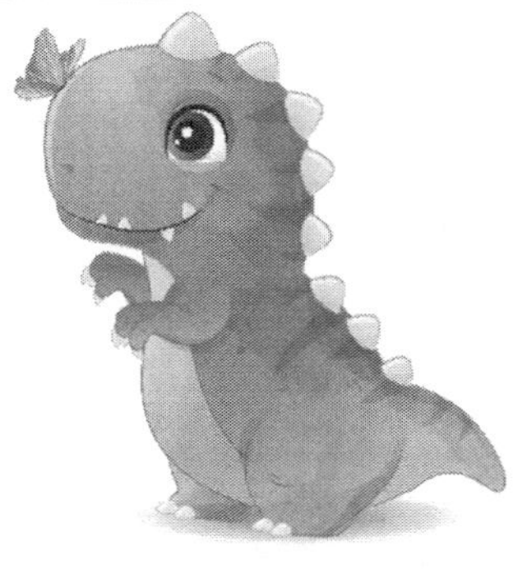

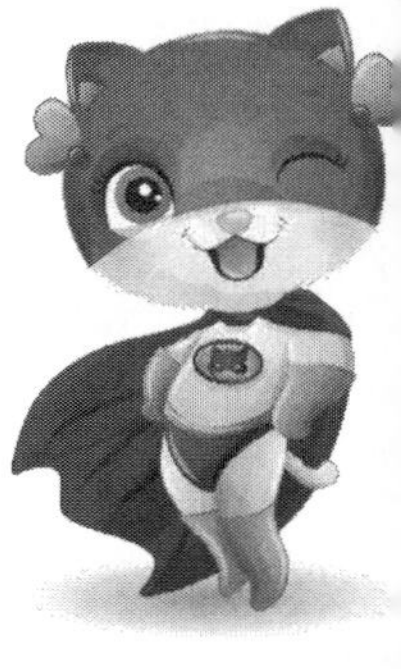

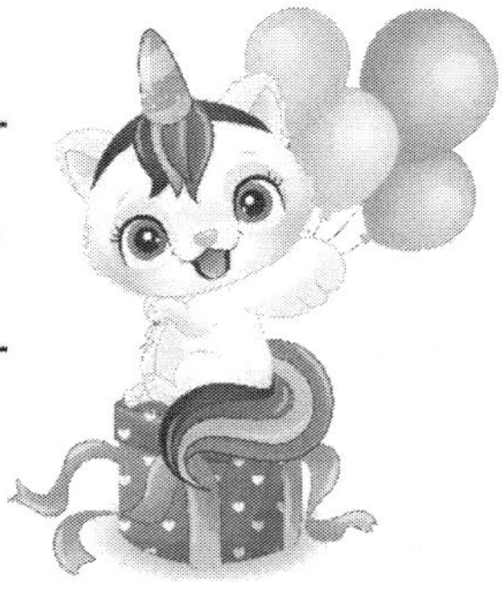

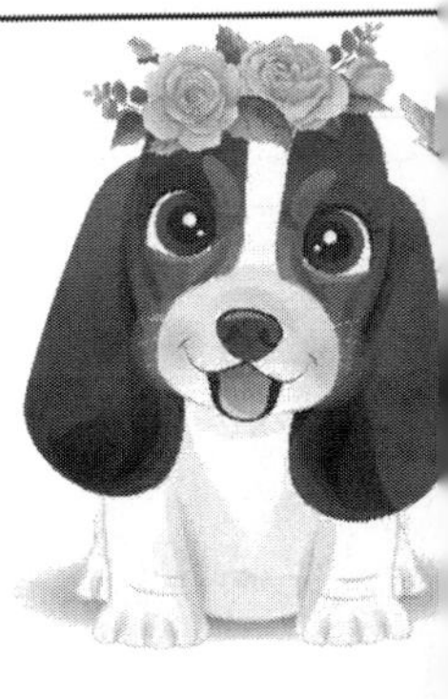

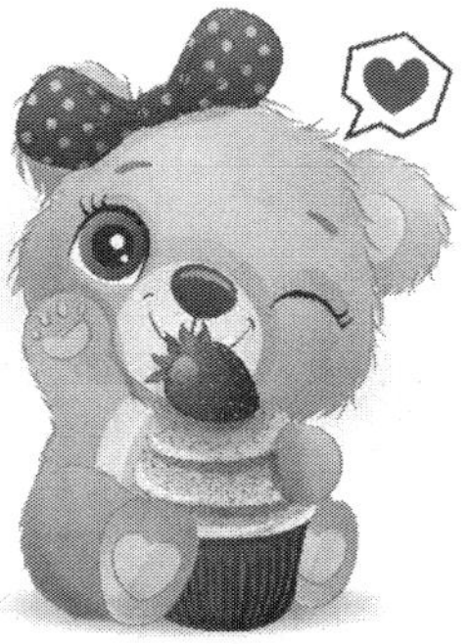

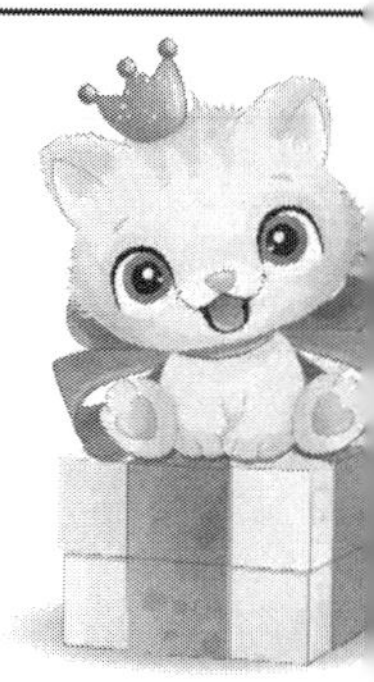

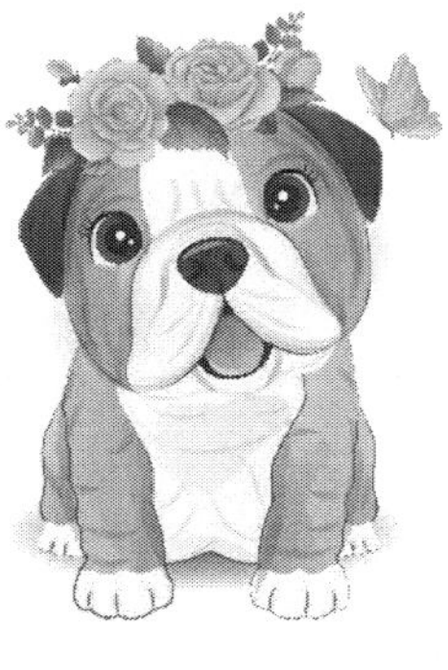

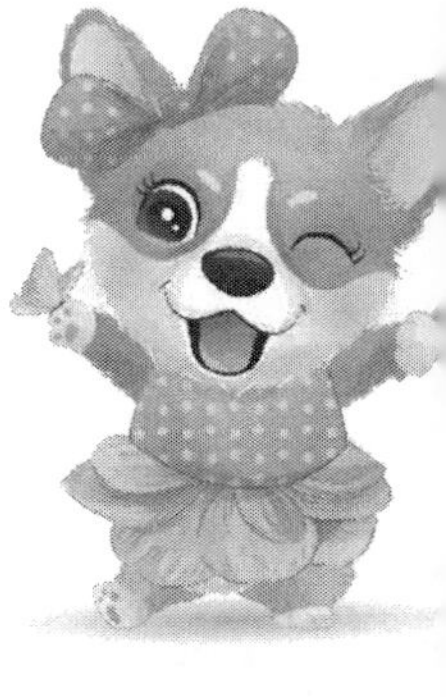

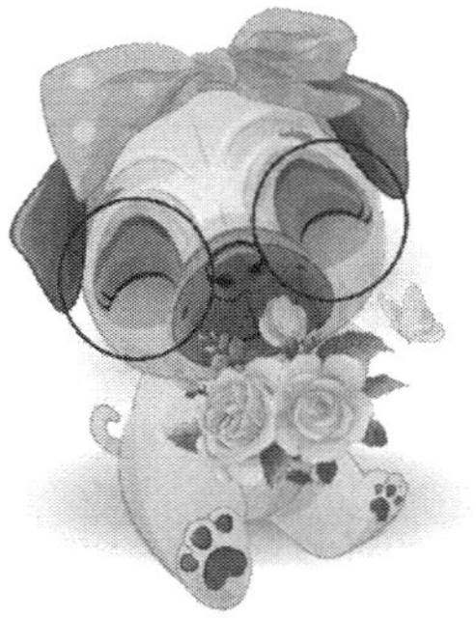

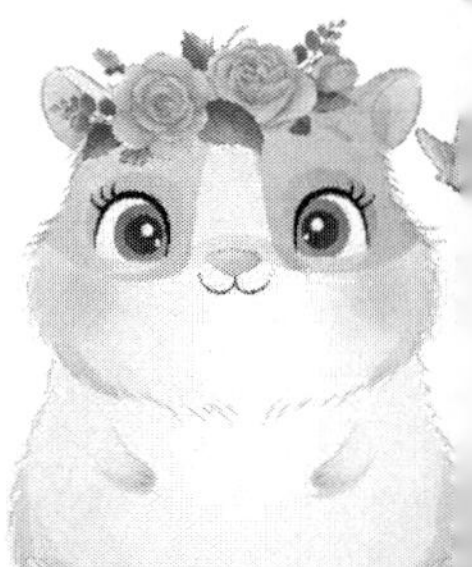

Lovely

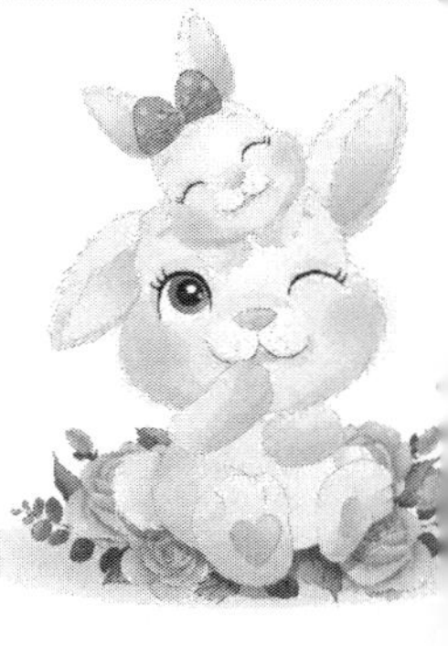

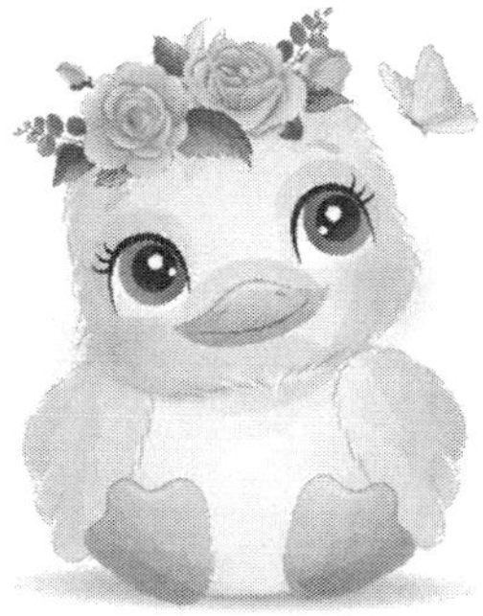

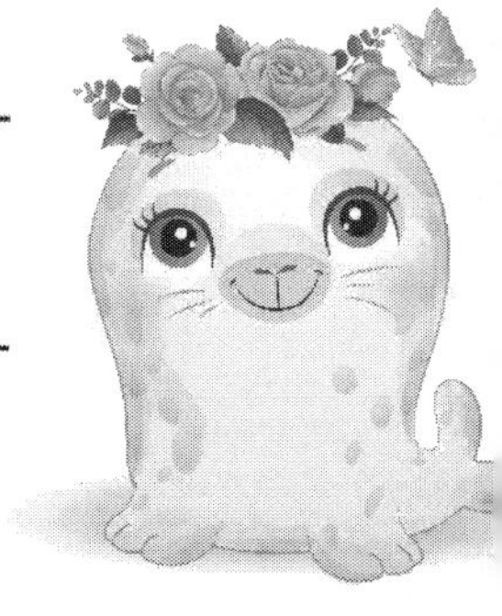

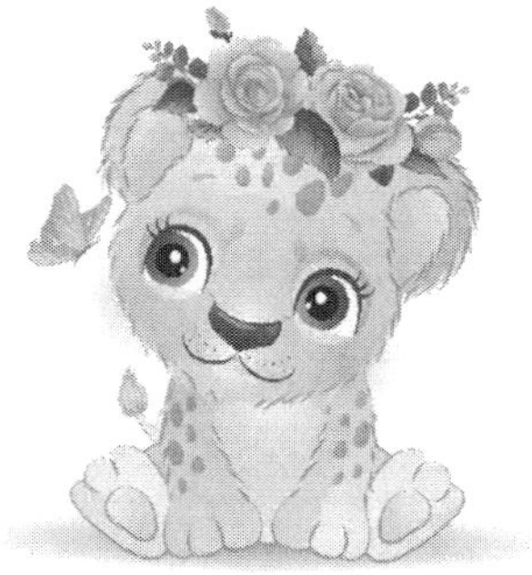

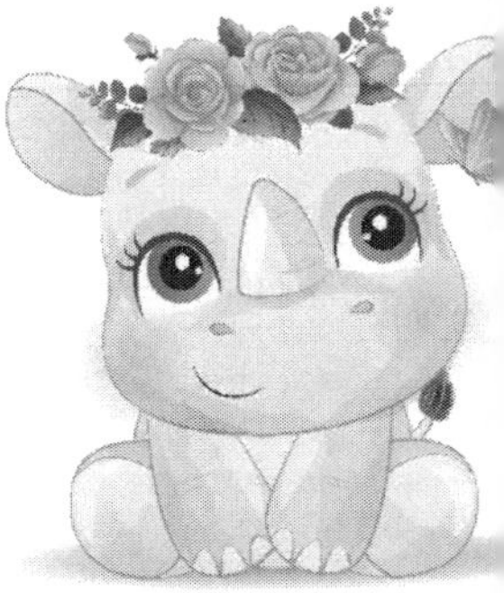

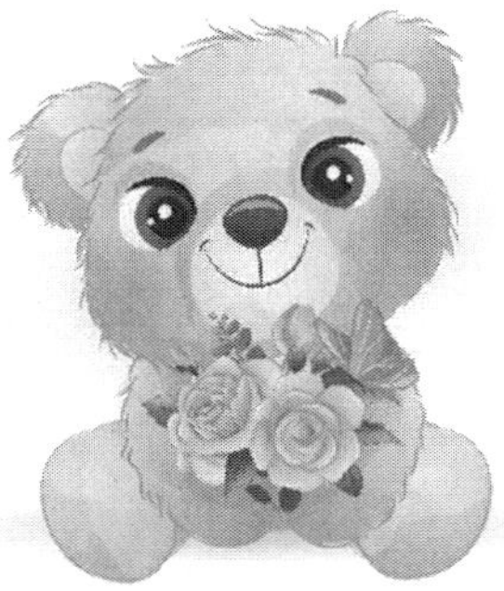

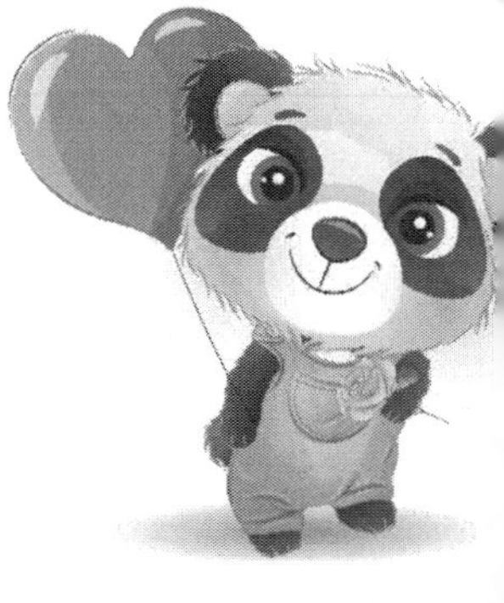

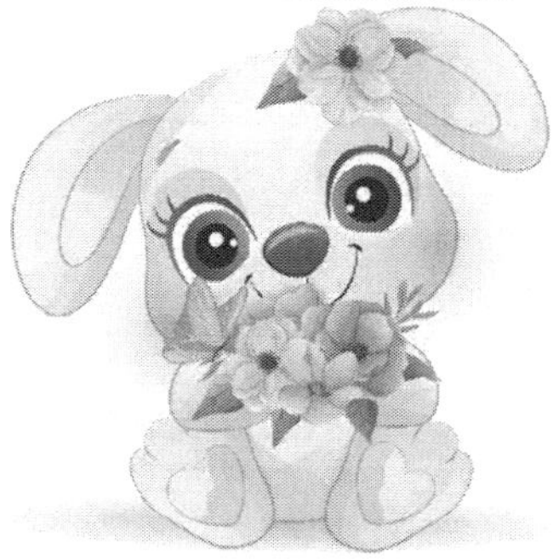

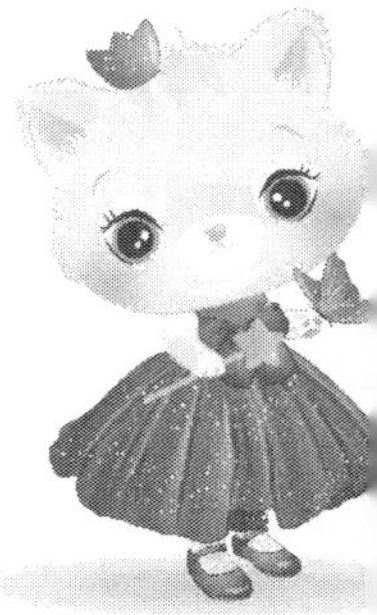

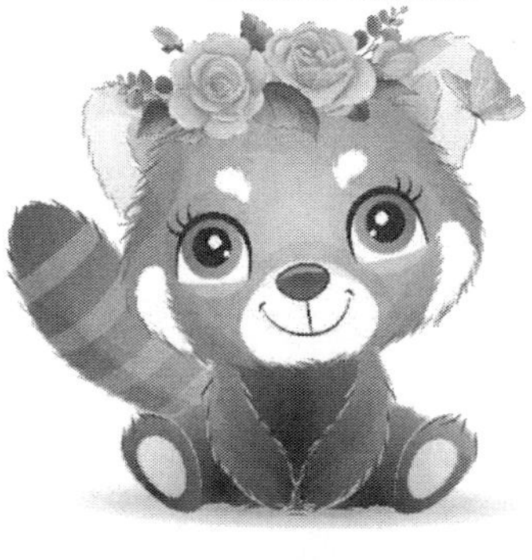

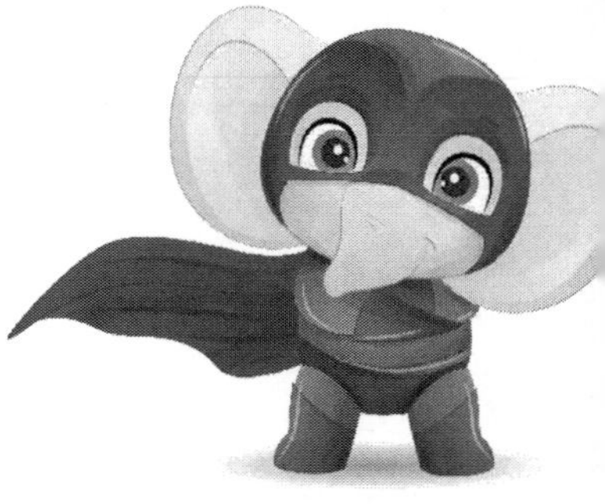

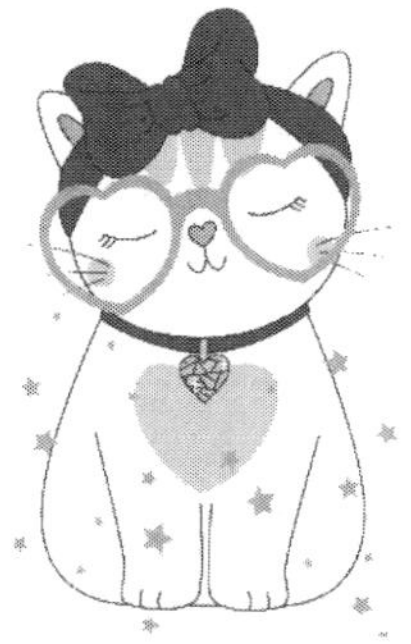

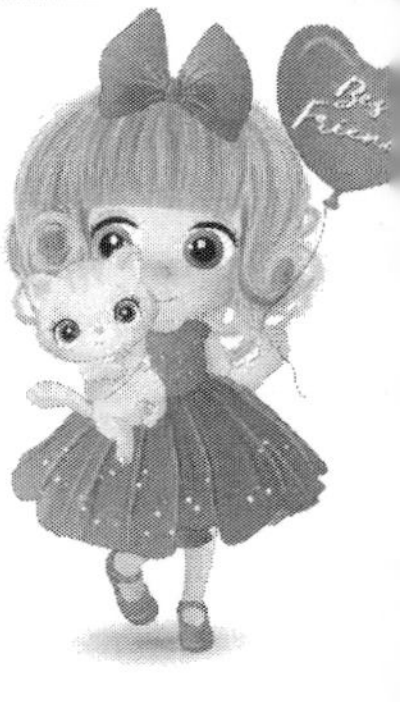

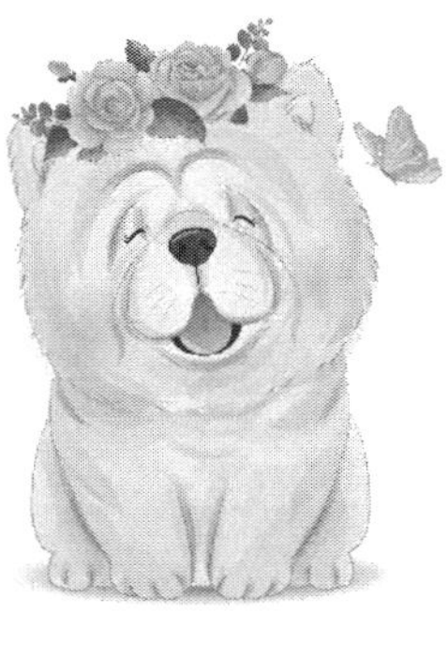

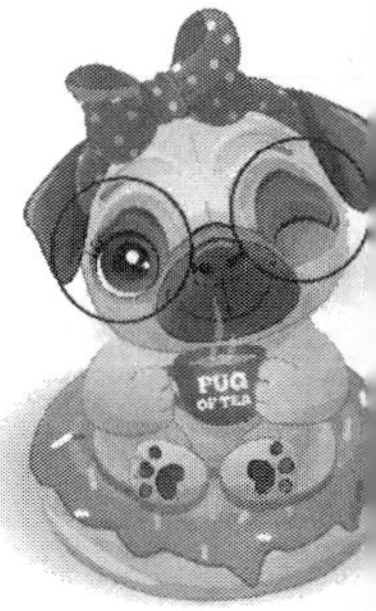

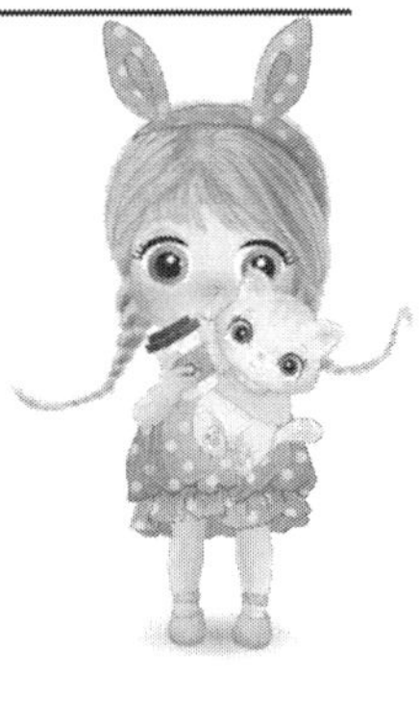

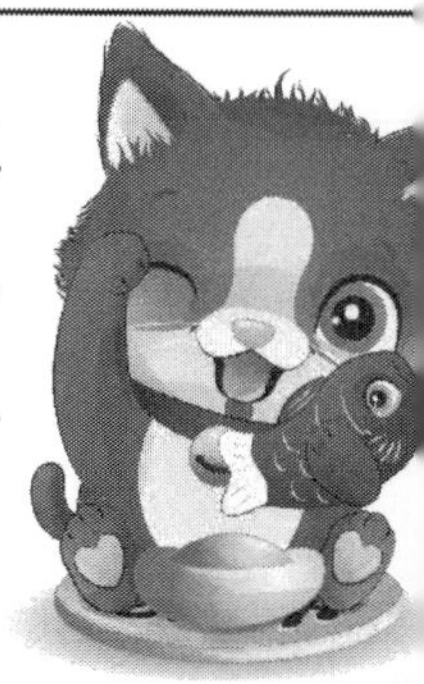